THE TENDERNESS OF THE WOLVES

THE TENDERNESS OF THE WOLVES

by Dennis Cooper

Introduction by Edmund White

 The Crossing Press, Trumansburg, NY 14886

Acknowledgements:

Some of these works have appeared in the following publications: *Alcatraz, Bachy, Barney, Beyond Baroque, Gay Sunshine, Hot Water Review, The L.A. Weekly, Little Caesar, Ouija Madness, Phone-A-Poem* (Boston), *Poetry Now, Soup, St. Marks Poetry Project Newsletter, Wet Magazine* and the anthology *Coming Attractions: American Poets in Their Twenties* (Little Caesar Press).

Cover Photograph by Jack Shear
Copyright © 1981, Jack Shear

Special thanks to Tim Dlugos, Michael Silverblatt and Jack Skelley.

Library of Congress Cataloging in Publication Data

Cooper, Dennis, 1953-
    The tenderness of the wolves.

    1. Homosexuality, Male--Literary collections.
I. Title.
PS3553.0582T4   811' .54   81-15104
ISBN 0-89594-066-3   AACR2
ISBN 0-89594-065-5 (pbk.)

for
Amy Gerstler

Table of Contents

Introduction

by Edmund White

Not long ago I berated in print the current college generation for its blandness and conservatism and lack of emotional and political acuteness. One of my students came up to me after reading those pages and said, "You know, we do feel things intensely, but we don't like to show it — I suppose we're just more refined than your generation."

This refinement is apparent everywhere in Dennis Cooper's new poems. It's not the usual sort; it isn't aristocratic or moral or cultural. But it is oddly esthetic, even epicurean. In a freeway and television culture that seems like so much featureless dreck to older Americans, the young have managed to detect purer shades of synthetic pink, finer plastic imitations. "He said 'Hi' to them, real intensely," is a line from The Tenderness of the Wolves; *one wonders whether one would have picked up the intensity. One of Cooper's poems is even called "The Blank Generation" but with no particular emphasis.*

In one sense the refinement of the blank generation consists in not selling anything. No moral lesson, no message, no political outcry, no personal plea, no artistic slogan — nothing is insisted on and the voice is never raised. Indeed, this is a world governed by style alone and that style's strongest injunction is: Never say or do anything embarrassing.

Of course, this sense of personal style and this fear of embarrassment are only a short step away from art and its proprieties — an art, to be sure, of the most narrow range though one in which every word, every gesture, registers. Even the fatalism, the inveterate drift of desire in these poems is true to the nature of art, since Nietzsche has taught us that "the will is the non-esthetic element par excellence." In a poetics (or life) so restricted, any slightest deviation will be sensed — in earthquake country not even the slightest tremor can be ignored.

But of course Dennis Cooper is not a naive member of the blank generation. He is its poet, its critic and its mimic. He has mastered its dialect, but when he speaks in it he tells us things we've never heard before, things we'd suspected but never articulated even to ourselves:

> I can't speak I'm so fucking stupid,
> Our bodies are simply stupendous.
> When we breathe, it takes us apart.
> You know. You're inside us.

In another poem, when a teenage boy and girl try sex for the first time, it "feels/ so cold and impressive to them." And in yet another, a fifteen-year-old hustler confides, "I was meant to be naked."

These sentiments are delicate because they are mumbled under the breath by someone whose handsome face is all scowls, fear and arrogance. These beautiful kids are scared and proud, too dumb to resist danger, too tactful to seek help. Their delicacy is all the more refined in "A Herd," the terrifying long prose poem that closes the book. I find this saga about a man who kills teenage boys comparable in its erotics of mutilation only to two films, In the Realm of the Senses and Salo. It is so painful and spooky and upsetting precisely because both the murderer and the murdered subscribe to the same code of refinement — a sullen aphasia that conceals and feeds a gnawing hunger for sensation. The man knows the boys will do anything for a drug high; he himself will do anything, including kidnap and murder, to secure a boy who will resemble one of his teen idols, "some ripe child whose hit songs were stuck on the radio's dials, whose visage beamed down from most billboards." The children of a mass culture create nothing, will nothing, reject nothing, declare nothing; they experience whatever is offered, including death at the end of a hypodermic needle.

William Carlos Williams long ago taught us that "The pure products of America go crazy" and that when they have sex they do so by "succumbing without/ emotion/ save numbed terror." Williams ends his poem with lines Cooper could well use as an epigraph: "No one/ to witness/ and adjust, no one to drive the car . . . "

Cooper, who grew up in Los Angeles and still lives there and is not yet thirty, surely knows the pure products of America. One of the teen mourners in "A Herd" is vexed when the father of a dead boy quotes *lyrics from the wrong pop song at his son's funeral: "How selfish of this man to pick a lyric which Jay didn't care about." Without Dennis Cooper, we would never have known about such eerie refinements being entertained behind the doped, handsome, expressionless face.*

1.

Then as Before

It was Saturday morning, so I could sleep in. But my body, used to the call of the high school, spaced-on at 7:15 and wouldn't be snuffed out again, no matter how much I yawned, on my stomach or back. So I propped a pillow behind me, sat up and let my eyes clear on the poster from Alain Resnais' *Providence,* hung on the back of my bedroom door. It was my favorite film. It held the right combination of smarts and emotion—starring the first, with a cameo by the latter. When I established myself as an artist and was handed a sizable budget, I'd do something like it.

On the top shelf of my book case, a neat row of film cans made up my oeuvre. I was still proud of maybe a third. I'd been making small epics since I was thirteen, when I'd ridden around on my Stingray bike shooting montages of where I hung out. I still tried to watch them and see where I'd been. I peered through the premature, wobbly art and they were trailers for my childhood, starring some friends who'd gone on to be strangers to me.

I leapt out of bed. I yanked a shoe box from the closet and cannonballed back in the covers. In the box was a stack of photos of me, my family and friends through my life. I dumped them out on the blanket and pawed through the mess for anything, anywhere, anyone special. There was myself, climbing out of some swimming pool. I was about ten years old. The less perfect color gradations in those days made me look gold, though I'd always been pale or burnt red.

Further back still, in black and white, one 8x10 featured me and some friends around eight years of age. We posed in a pack outside an old theatre (torn down since then) having just seen or about to see something. The photo's frame cut off below the marquee and in at both sides from the cases with posters, so I couldn't tell what my tastes were like then. My friends looked like typical children, with faces too mushy to give a clue what they were thinking. I remembered I thought I could tell.

I almost knew this old world where the ornate tail end of my parents' Montclair (lower right corner) would speed down this avenue pointing at places I could still picture—a Ralph's Supermarket, my lime-green grade school, my family's first Spanish style home. I wanted to locate these other young fellows whose parents had dragged them to some Amnesiaville. But I could only squint at their faces beyond the grid of the photo, as if through the chain length fence of a school yard, scanning that shrunken-up hiding place. Now I looked at the light on the photo, then out the window which threw it—a playground more teasing than this tiny, flashbulb-lit one I had come from. Then as before, I had no choice in the matter. I put on my clothes and went out there.

There

He stood alone in the shadow.
His hands and his shoes jutted
out of the dark, with some dope
smoke. The rest of his body was
vague but exact, like a hologram
glimpsed through thick glasses.

He had two or three friends who
took orders, strolled off and
came back with treasures. His
calm seemed as great as the one
in cartoons so deep in his past
they'd grown soft and unlined.

It was enough. Punks, jocks,
everyone watched him, pictured
him sprawled at a desk, clothes
torn apart by ulterior powers,
his sneer smudged with girls'
kisses, boys' wet red fists.

Somehow one girl got to him,
towed him around. He leaned
on her body. They grew loaded
together, mouths swinging open,
and walked in a slight pas de
deux on the outskirts of things.

Now they linger behind their
old friends, wiser but slower,
hugging in backgrounds, staring
into some nowhere, their eyes
grey with rest and the kind of
lust only the bored can imagine.

They loll around in their
arms and the look on his face
makes both whisper, undress.
Then they touch where they've
always imagined, and it feels
so cold and impressive to them.

Being Aware

Men are drawn to my ass by
my death-trance blue eyes
and black hair, tiny outfit,
while my father is home with
a girl, moved by the things
I could never think clearly.

Men smudge me onto a bed,
drug me stupid, gossip and
photograph me till I'm famous
in alleys, like one of those
jerk offs who stare from
the porno I sort of admire.

I'm fifteen. Screwing means
more to the men than to me.
I daydream right through it
while money puts chills on
my arms, from this to that
grip. I was meant to be naked.

Hey, Dad, it's been like this
for decades. I was always
approached by your type, given
dollars for hours. I took a
deep breath, stripped and they
never forgot how I trembled.

It means tons to me. Aside
from the obvious heaven
when cumming, there's times
I'm with them that I'm happy
or know what the other guy
feels, which is progress.

Or, nights when I'm angry,
if in a man's arms moving
slowly to the quietest music—
his hands on my arms, in my
hands, in the small of my back
take me back before everything.

Wednesday

"The point is to touch them," a coach says, and eyes the young men on the field. They are throwing balls and looking around for directions. He lifts one big hand and waves it at them. "Hold your horses."

". . . and in doing so make them grow up," frowns another. He's been in the war, seen how boys either cut it or don't in the big time. "One fall on their asses won't rape them."

Off a short distance, girls flop around in their sweatshirts and shorts, led onto the basketball court for some sit-ups, to disco. Their eyes are more calm than the boys', especially turned to each other. They talk about creeps, those on the field for example.

The girls' coach is tired of their laziness. They'll do the exercise right, and with vigor. Her whistle clicks in her teeth, then squeals until all eyes are hers. "Now," she says, "Let's get going. Lie on your backs. . .bend your legs up. . .and touch them."

When a single bell rings the boys and girls drop what they're holding, rush into two dressing rooms, slide out of blue shorts and shout. Some trot to the showers. A few are too nervous to bathe in front of the others.

At the far end of the boys' locker room an open door leads to an office. Inside, coaches are wrestling. One of them leans in the doorway. A naked kid raps to him, voice full of reverence and fear. The coach keeps his gaze on the ceiling. Anything the boy says is so moving.

The student, Steve Behr, is stupid but handsome. At this point he pulls it off. His parents like him and friends run the gamut from poets to robbers. "A nice guy," they say when girls ask what The Behr's like. "He's decent."

Both Jocelyn and Brenda, two lanky blondes, like Steve. In their locker room they dash to the showers, side by side, talking about him. Joc loves his haircut and Bren thinks his peak was last summer, so suntanned they hardly could recognize him. He said "Hi" to them, real intensely.

The boys' coaches know what Steve has and hasn't. He's a good looking boy and a friendly guy. Fine at athletics, tries had. They notice him sprawled in the showers. He sees them staring and grins, but he can't imagine their feelings. Some asshole just slugged him and he fell down on his ass. But by this time it's nothing.

Grouped outside the gymnasium, students wait for the bell to ring. Then they meet their friends at the usual places. Druggies stroll toward the restrooms. Jocks jog by the bleachers. Girls are scattered among and beyond them.

When Steve looks at the girls he doesn't know what to do. So, he has picked a lover from those who are like him, for whatever reason. They meet up and walk toward the street as a couple, keds flattening the grass. The yellow buses open their doors and students climb in. Windows fill up with steam.

At home Steve's mother works in the garden all day, and waits for her son. Or she cleans up the house, or looks out a window. Her breath leaves a cloud on the glass. Now she sees him come walking up the black driveway, scanning the place till he spies her. The look on her face is familiar.

They meet in the kitchen—she with her coffee cup, he with a spoon draped in ice cream. She lays out her day on the table. He mentions his between swallows, then jumps on his gold ten speed bike and whizzes down Fair Street to a friend's house, as he has every Wednesday since grade school.

Kevin's parents have money. Their backyard is like arboretums that Steve has been bussed to on field trips and, in its damp depths, as shady as though they were tinted-in grey, the gardener's store room sits open. Once inside it, Steve draws out a joint from his wallet, lights its tip, lets it simmer a second then slurps the smoke down. He hands it to Kevin.

When the small room is clouded and their tension's snuffed like the cherry, they strip and lie out on the cold cement floor, cocks nearly branding each other between them. Then Steve pulls away and they shoot their white loads on the ground.

They smear it around with their heels, and slip back into tee-shirts plus jeans. Kevin's shirt says, "Surf Life!" on its chest and Steve's holds the colored-in face of a rock star who both of them worship. They wish they could kiss him right now.

While walking back to the mansion, Kevin looks in Steve's eyes. They're just calm, nothing special. Now the house is in sight and a woman leans out of a lower right window, watching the sunset. "Staying for dinner?" she calls out to Steve. Kevin asks him more gently. "Okay," Steve whispers, then cups his mouth with his hands. "Okay!"

John Kennedy Jr. Faces the Future

"Well," he says, "What's ahead?"
and wipes Michelob from his chin.
His friends nod, drunker than he is.
He has been blathering for hours.
". . . and where will *I* be, you know?
Parents and all that, just bore me."

Someone suggests a political office.
"Too obvious," he says. How about
a race car driver? "I haven't got
the guts." An actor. "Well, maybe."
A writer. "Slight possibility." A
lawyer. "Those guys are assholes."

The girl in his arms says, "Be
practical. As long as you have
wealth you can just lounge around.
Why fuck with your legend? All
this talk is boring. It doesn't
get you anywhere. It's bullshit."

John stands up from the table,
walks outside alone. "Let him go,"
a pal mumbles. He strolls through
the streets of Hyannis, wandering,
thinking. He is so alone in this.
No one else could ever understand.

He wants to read his name outside
the society column, find people who
will notice him. But his thoughts are
messy, too drunken, and he sits down
on a lone park bench, his big wavy
head in hands, the whole world in them.

Hustlers

for Jerry Patterson

Two beers screw my head up.
I lean back against a dark wall.
My long hair drifts in my eyes.
Let's say the moon makes a decision.
I land the corner legend surrounds.
I say more than I pretend to.
I prefer to be fucked to The Beatles.
I stand with the guys I resemble.
Jerry, Tom, Dick, Sam, Julian, Max, Timmy.
Guess which of those names is perfect.
We dream of a casual million.
We light our cigarettes gently.
I take what the night has to offer.
I roll a ripe peach from one wrist to the other.
I can't speak I'm so fucking stupid.
Our bodies are simply stupendous.
When we breathe, it takes us apart.
You know. You're inside us.

Lunch

A portable Sony taperecorder was set on a bench in the high school's quad. One of five kids who pow-wowed around it had made a tape of the latest 45 records from England.

June wore a huge, untucked white button-down shirt over red plastic pants from a cheap Halloween costume she'd picked up at Woolworth's. She'd reinforced them at the seams with electrician's tape. Today's array of buttons, military-ish in a clump on her right breast pocket, included two slogans: *I want complete control* (an oldie) and *I just give up* (a newie), plus buttons sporting rock bands' names—one of which was famous, two of which were obscure. One handmade badge was emblazoned with the name of her boyfriend's band, Nix. They were still at the rehearsal stage.

Jim, unlike tubby June, had the blessing of a scrawny frame on which he could hang nearly anything. He sported a traditional tweed coat which he'd wadded up and rested a dictionary on all night, and pants that ran out of cotton six inches from his Beatle boots, showing thin hairy legs and skeletal ankles. His teeshirt had red and pink splotches asplash it. His black hair had been recently crewcut to match the look worn by the hot new British band Madness, which had just been through town. Jim's face had held thick glasses for twelve years, but he couldn't find a place for them with this outfit. He put up with a blurred world today and looked somewhat perplexed.

Kick and Xeeman—names they'd taken on like Mohammedans, in their bows to fashion—were a couple who'd moved out of their parents' house to live together. Kick made some money designing clothes at a shop called Vertigo Fashions. That, plus Xeeman's allowance, kept them in suitably meager meals, homemade clothes and at the feet of most rock stars. They clung by each other, impassive behind Ray Charles-type dark glasses. She nodded to a song's beat. He wouldn't let himself.

Sam was a kid they let linger around. He hadn't taken on fashion as yet, except for the marginally "hip" Bowie button clipped to his teeshirt. But he was as enthusiastic as any of them about the new music. Before he'd joined them he'd been the unwilling sparring partner of dumb jocks who didn't like unclassifiables. This crowd took him in for his own protection, as much as anything else.

The tape rolled past songs which were all noise, and ones which held melodies. Each were hip at the moment. As they came on, talk turned to the artists, their latest records, possible tour and importance to all mankind's future.

"I still say," Xeeman yawned, "that Magazine is the biggest hope. Their last two albums didn't live up to the first one, but with a guy like Howard Devoto at their helm, who has an IQ of 140, you know they've got something."

From the tape recorder, Devoto accompanied her: "Time flies," he intoned in a deep, broken wail, "time crawls, like an insect up and down the walls."

"They could pull out of their slump," Jim reasoned, "but bands coming up now using those fierce dancable beats are making the biggest impression. If any of them ever grow wits on their rhythms they could do wonders."

"Your admiration for their proposal is well documented," Kick said, eyeing Jim's haircut. Kick had a tendency toward pretension, but it, his friends knew, had its place.

The songs jerked on and off, one after another. The crowd listened and strained their eyes on the other students around, in their own cliques and couples, kissing or scolding or regaling each other.

June slumped on the bench, letting her posture slope, then slide until she fell on the ground.

"I need speed!" she bellowed. Then, feeling inspired, "Speed is what I need!"

Sam laughed. The others looked tolerant, knowing her. She got up and brushed off her pants.

"Got any electronic stuff on that?" She pointed at the recorder.

"On the other side," Jim said. "We've got time. We'll get there."

"Here comes Jack!" Xeeman was surprised. "Oh," she said shyly to Kick, "you don't know him."

"Xeeman," Jack smiled. "Hi. How are you?"

"Fine. I haven't seen you since, well...since our last party. I don't think I ever introduced you to Kick, the guy I live with."

Jack stuck out his hand. Kick shook it rigidly, once up then down. He was suspicious. Who was this guy?

"Jack is a filmmaker. An amazing talent," Xeeman told her friends.

"Did you see Beth B and Scott B's *Black Box*?" Jim asked Jack. He was speaking of a film which a young couple in New York had made, about the torture of a young man. Its ambivalent sadism had made it famous.

"Yeah. It was kind of interesting but it didn't live up to the hype."

"I loved it," Jim said and rolled his eyes at Kick who narrowed his in sympathy.

24

Sam, seeing a chance to look smart, asked, "Ever seen any Fellini? I have. He's really something."

The gang looked embarrassed.

"Yes. I've seen his films," Jack nodded diplomatically, and turned back to Xeeman. "The reason I came over is that I'm making a film and wondered whether, if you have a few minutes, you'd be in it? See, I'm taking my friends and turning a camera on them, asking a question and having them answer it for two and a half minutes, until the film runs out."

"What question?" Kick wanted to know.

"The person can't know until I turn the camera on. Everyone gets the same one. It's a surprise. That's part of the point. So, Xeeman, would you do it?"

Xeeman genuinely liked Jack's films and, although it sounded like a situation of possible embarrassment, she was honored to be asked. "Well, okay. Now?"

"Yes. Come with me and we'll go over by the Metal Shop. No one will be around there. I'll have you back in ten minutes."

She turned to Kick. "I'll be right back."

"Obviously." He sounded annoyed.

"Look,' Xeeman said, "I've known Jack a long time and this is something I want to do."

"Just go," June smirked. "Fuck Kick."

Kick sneered at June.

"Go," he sighed.

Jack had Xeeman stand with her back to the orange stucco building. Her red clothes looked vibrant against it. He handed her a microphone and peered through the camera until his friend was in focus. He pulled the trigger and film rolled.

"Xeeman," he pronounced clearly, "Talk about yourself."

"Talk about myself? God...Well, I'm seventeen. I go to this school, Orville Wright High School in West Los Angeles, California. I live with a boyfriend of mine named Kick...Christ, what's there to say? Hmmm...I like clothes, as you can tell. My favorite bands are Magazine, Wire, Pere Ubu...umm...Public Image and a few others. I like the intellectual ones. Music's very important to me now, unlike when you and I hung around a lot, Jack. Back then I mainly read books, as I recall. I guess I've changed a lot since those days...God, that's probably taken fifteen seconds or something. How much time do I have left...You don't tell?...You don't talk at all?...Okay, well, I don't know what to say, really...I don't have any big plans for my life at the moment. Kick might get famous as a fashion designer and we could move to New York or London and see all the best groups and meet people like Warhol...I used to draw but I don't anymore, except when I'm on the phone and that sort of shit...This is impossible...umm...Things are strange around here. I mean at school. There's some kind of muderer who killed a hippie kid. A couple of other boys haven't shown up lately. Everyone's talking about it, you know, like 'Who's next?' and 'Is he one of us or someone we know?'...It's something to gossip about, but it's got everyone...well, I guess I should only talk for myself. I'm spooked. But that doesn't have much to do with me...I just don't know what to say, Jack. Why are you making this film? Oh, you can't talk...I guess it'll be pretty interesting to see this and learn what I'm like and what everyone's like...Well, I'm sorry I'm not talking more about me. I'm going to light a cigarette. That's something I do...Now I inhale. Now I exhale. That's me all over...When this is finished I'll go back to my friends and finish listening to a tape of new music. Oh, my friends are Jim, June, Kick and Sam. They're who I see mostly these days. They look relatively normal while my friends and I try to look abnormal. Except now our look is chic so I guess we should do something else, but I don't know what that would be. Besides, Kick needs..."

The film ran out.

"That's it," Jack announced. He rolled the microphone cord up and put the camera back in its black case.

"Jack, that's a pretty strange experience being on the spot like that. What have people been doing?"

"Everyone acts differently. There's no right or wrong way to respond. It's all interesting and revealing."

"Well, you'll let me see it, of course. And let's get together sometime and see a concert or something. I miss being with you."

"Me too, definitely."

She waved and strolled back to her friends.

Jack checked off a list in his notebook. Four down and fifteen to shoot. So far it was going well.

My Parents

grew up in Montana, on ranches
in barns I held my big nose in
on summer vacation. The sun
in Montana is heaven and hell.
I dove from it into the bluest
water I've seen, then crawled
back onto a riverbank fresh
from the oven and slept till
my father called like a coyote
over the fields, to go home.

My mother lived on a shady
street, in a mansion where
ceilings were so high up that
I felt as if I was outdoors
when the house lights were off.
My grandmother dressed up a
store room for her in its
depths with balloons, ribbons
orange as the tips of lit
fuses, wrapping her boxes of

toys. I lay out alone on a
bed that smelled like a slice
of a wedding cake, fell asleep
there, fingering dolls iced
with dust. I had a ten gallon
hat squished down over my head.
Now it sits like a dixie cup
on my hair, my parents are old
and those places are surely
torn down. When I ask them
about it they shake little

fists. They say it was empty,
filled with an odor which
science has cleaned off the
earth. And, with those words,
they look like they'd sniffed
where a kitchen door opened a
crack then followed its warm

sweet whiff to a den, in two
chairs, facing a wall that's as
white as the snow which has
covered and chilled that world.

For Mark Stephens

My mother drank, and she sat
in a house the size of the Hilton
in one small room, at a black
grand piano, through cigarette
smoke, by a dinner so old it
cracked like dried mud. A tune
created her mood. Some whim
was letting her play the same
exercise seventeen times. She
had been smart in the Fifties.
She was not handsome, but she
was composed, made me between
vodkas. My room was up one
or more of the stairways, left
down the hall, left again. I
knelt here, twisted a knob and
rock music rose genie-like in
the room, gripped me and took
me away. I'd leap in my room,
hand strumming my belt like a
rock star, lip-synching what
hid my new thoughts in my body.
When my sister split, there
were places to hide in the
mansion. Piles of her junk
became far distant planets.
I couldn't quite build a
transporter, though I hung up
black lights, sheets over
lamps, played songs at half-speed.
I thought if I darkened
the room, blurred sofas, sat
there, that might be heaven,
controlled by one light switch
like LSD hinted. Hearing a
song, I went up. Downstairs
my mother got drunk all alone.
Knowing that I was nearby she
would wobble to the piano,
plop down and play the one
piece she learned from lessons,

her body bent forward, with
spit on her lips, eyes shining.
The melody rose through her
clutches, was part of the world
that corraled where even her
hands couldn't snuff it. The
music sank through the ceiling
to where I'd crouch dreaming,
host to the tingle of darkness.
It touched in a way I couldn't
shrug off. Doped, far away
from my life, I listened, and
it reached out and caressed me.

My Past

for Jim Stegmiller

is a short string of beautiful
boys or young men I admired,
dragged to bed, left in ruins
on corners with taxi fare home.
Another of friends who were
horny, who I could have slept
with but didn't because they
were ugly, insane or too much
like me to be sexy. We were
partners for sweeps of wild
parties, took dope till they felt
like museums which we
could pick-over for bodies
to idealize with caresses.
The sun rose slowly. I was
still huffing and toiling
with them, like a sculptor
attempting to get things just
right—finally collapsing
in bed with some smeared,
smelly torso before me, and
a powerful wish to be left
alone. Take you, for example,
who I found throwing-up in
the bathroom of some actor's
mansion and crowned my new
boyfriend. Your ass made me
nervous till I explored it.
Now I want to forget it. My
friends feel this way too.
I know them. We've been close
since before we were artists
working to leave haunted eyes
on our lovers. I've thrown
out hundreds like you, and
found only art can remain so
aloof in its make-up that I'll
stare endlessly into its eyes
like a kid with a microscope.

Once I was back when art chatted
just over my head, when I was
still glancing up the red swim
trunks of some boy who I think
was named Jimmy, and wondering
what could be out there, miles
from my hands. He was leaving
like you. Who knows where that
man and that feeling are now.

For My Birthday

After much talk and laughter
friends are buying a whore,
one I couldn't worm from
the bars with a toothy smile.
He will be fairly beautiful.
They have shopped the foul
alleys of Selma, finding red
hair and eyes with dark powers.
On the night of my birth I'll
proceed to a particular motel.
At an appointed moment someone
will knock two times and enter.
It will be my gift, paid up
until morning, and I'll try
to talk with him first, then
just give up and rattle him
orders that he'll understand
or embellish, teaching me love
the easy way: arms obligated
to take me, repaying each kiss,
caressing by reflex. I'll be
nice to him, hoping he might
contract my desire, knowing he'll
ditch me when his watch strikes
day, anxious for a real fuck or
someone who speaks his language,
as dull and slurred as that is.

Abba

for Brad Gooch

We snort all our coke
on the way to the party.
We bring the new album.
We dance while we listen.

The band is two women
whose husbands control them.
They do not speak our language.
Each syllable's an obstacle.

They are in love with a man.
He is in love with another.
But they're in no hurry.
They could wait forever.

And when they are out
on the make for a lover,
they'll always find him.
They are the tigers.

We are too stoned to.
We dance till we're tired
and listen to lyrics
we mouth like a language.

What we feel, when we
hear them, is inexpressible.
We can't put it in words.
Maybe our dances show it.

Abba lives for their music.
We long for each other.
They see what we're doing.
They put it on record.

They play it, we listen.
We are absolutely stunned.
We feel, and they know
more than anyone can say.

Drugs

A friend dies one night,
swallows too many pills
on his way to a party
and grows pale as dust
in a shaft of moonlight.
You long to reach him
again, all your life.
A priest says you'll
find him in the future
under cover of death;
you will stand and sing
near his glowing side.
We tell you to join us,
get loaded, forget him.
One day you shoot so
much stuff you fall over.
You hope to see him but
only grow clammy, more
stupid, like someone on
quaaludes. Now you and
he walk the same clouds
only when we've been
stoned and think back
on our lives, full of
dead bodies, and bright
now as heaven behind us.

Dinner

"What a beautiful ass," said the man with the brown mustache to the man with the blond one. "...like the Blarney Stone or a chunk of the Wailing Wall. I'd like to fall there and..." What he meant to say was that here was an ass which he'd love to find in his bed, lift the sheet up like a tent flap on heaven, and feel it there, peaceful and warm.

Tom stood at the counter, feeding beer into his nerves. He'd driven by this barroom for years. Recently, he'd heard via gossip at school that it had a gay clientele. Tonight he'd been in his room, trying to get his mind off a blond in his Geography class. He'd grown pissed at himself for just sitting there jerking off and, in that anger's slight bravery, drove here.

The bar was crowded but, scanning its realm, he couldn't see anyone his age. He'd hoped he would see someone from his college, a guy he had wondered about. Not even male cheerleaders were here, though a handful of guys on the small, strobing dance floor had their backs to him and might wind up familiar when they whirled around.

"I want him," stated the brown mustache to the blond one, after panning around their quarters once more to make sure there was no competition. His eyes lounged on Tom.

"Yeah," the blond smirked, "you and the legions." He pointed there, there and there at men ogling.

"I have my powers," smiled the brunette, and he sauntered in Tom's direction.

A few dances later, Tom followed his partner into the parking lot, to a white Cadillac off by itself at the back of the building, near its trash bins. He couldn't tell for sure in the dark, but the car's windows looked tinted, which would make sense, to hide what had surely been done in there night after night. He breathed deeply, trying to cure a slight case of the shakes.

The man unlocked the door, opened it and gestured him inside. He stepped past the polite, chauffeur-like posture, the extended arm, the pointing hand, and slid across the velour back seat to the opposite side. His foot hit a bottle of something down on the floor. The man climbed in after, and reached over to make sure the locks were secure on both doors. Then he fumbled down by the young man's feet and came up with the bottle.

"Some vodka?" He tipped it at Tom.

They traded it back and forth a few times in a charged silence, while the man scrutinized him and he tried, with a toss of his head, to look casual. When the bottle was empty, there was nothing between them.

The man tongued his ear. "Let's get your pants off," he whispered.

Tom lifted his hips. The man pulled the jeans down over his feet. He ripped off the tennies, then Tom reached down and peeled his own socks.

He felt the man's mouth on his cock, which was still only semi-erect. "This should get it hard for sure," he thought. But the man did everything this side of biting it off and it still drooped away.

Tom looked down and saw that the man was staring at him with a vague question in his eyes. Tom didn't know how to answer it so he said, "It's okay. Just get what you want. I don't mind."

The man relaxed a few seconds, kissing the softening penis, absent-mindedly rubbing Tom's legs. He wondered whether to try and give the boy pleasure in some other way, or just go ahead with his game plan. The kid was an angel. He had long, lightly haired legs and was practically porcelain everywhere else. The body was trim and, glancing up at Tom's eyes, which were looking somewhere else, thinking impenetrable things, he confirmed how pretty the face was.

"Okay. Why don't you get on your hands and knees, facing your window. Do you know the position I mean?"

Feeling calm now, Tom pulled off his shirt. He squatted and turned so his ass and legs extended lengthwise over the seat. He shifted until he felt comfortable, pressed one hand flat to the seat pad below and one to the side of the car.

He felt the man's hands on the soles of his feet, working their way up his legs, combing those fields for his soft spot. His forehead rested against the window. Looking outside, he saw a man walk alone to a car and unlock its door. The small inner lights made it seem warmly intricate there, like a carnival seen from a distance. The stranger folded away inside it. He and it darkened. The car glided away.

Tom stared at the trash cans. A Kellogg's Corn Flakes box had fallen out. He gazed at the untended back of the building as carefully as he imagined anyone ever had, aside from its architect.

The man ran his hands up the boy's legs. The handsome young face was away and the man had only this form to admire, with his impression of the boy's looks, their possible expression, to give the torso importance enough to do what he wanted. The ass was impeccable. The man would kiss here without having to worry about its opinion. Nothing would watch him or pull back or twitch beyond recognition. The boy was as distant from these moves as God from His priests down on earth.

Tom stared at but didn't see the armrest. He flipped the ashtray lid open and shut, unthinkingly. He'd come around. This felt sexy. He looked back over his shoulder. At the end of his back, the man's haughty veneer had become ugly and hyperactive. The eyes bugged. Everything on his face sloped, like the sides of a volcano, out to the mouth. It reminded Tom of the face of a desperate swimmer who he once had felt clawing by in the ocean, flailing up toward fresh air.

He turned to the window again. His cock was hard and one of his hands pumped it harder. He could imagine the blond in his class was behind him, doing this with eyes as fierce and a tongue as sharp as a lion's.

The smokey glass was a voluptuous white with Tom's breath. He licked it away, kept tonguing the glass, the upholstery, bit the armrest so hard that stuffing showed in his teethmarks.

The man was up on his knees now, slapping Tom's ass as if it were o.d.ing, fucking it with three greasy fingers, twisting the balls like the rotary on a toy airplane. Both the men's breaths blew in ever altering rhythms, manned by the shapes of words which, because of the distance between them, neither could quite comprehend.

Tom's head bumped the window over and over. He was dreaming of two or three guys back there on his ass, all of them crazy for him, having been lowered to that. He pushed his tongue out as far as it reached, licked all around his big lips.

The man felt hog wild, like he always had at these moments. The boy's ass was as red as a stoplight. He wanted further inside. He unfolded a palm from his cock, fished the popper out of his shirt pocket, reached under Tom's nose and cracked it.

"Sniff in hard."

The boy did, until his upper legs tensed, which showed it had worked. Now the man churned three fingers deeper into the well-stretched-out hole, withdrew them a little and pushed four back in. He squeezed the thumb up. Then he dialed and dialed until his hand was enclosed. The anus handcuffed his wrist. The boy was breathing so deeply the man thought that he might be dangerous or in danger.

Suddenly, Tom shot off on his fingers. His body shuddered. His head clunked forward against the glass.

Now the man worked his own cock, concentrating his thoughts on the fact that his hand was inside of a beautiful boy. In a flash, he came all over the seat. Then he screwed his hand out. His breathing slowed to its tempo. He looked at what he had done.

"Sit up, okay?" he asked.

Tom obeyed.

The man eyed the boy's face impassively, as he might a Miss Texas contestant. He felt like he'd held it under some water until it confessed what he'd needed. What beauty it held was deeper set than its bones now, plowed under all the man's knowledge.

Tom reached for his clothes and started untangling, wiping his hands with the wad of them, swabbing his neck.

The man gripped his shoulder, whispered, "Put on your things and take off. I'm going for a walk." Then he opened the door and was gone, in a roll of the evening's air that covered Tom's body with goose bumps, until the door slammed.

The Blank Generation

for Rik L. Rik

The future fills you
in with a question.
You answer, "Death,"
get your face on the
lid of SLASH Magazine.

It's as if someone
unchained your hands.
You scratch yourself.
You break a bottle
on your head onstage

and get popular fast.
Kids like to watch
you more than movies
then they're bored
no matter what you do.

You hate them all.
You speak their minds
writing poems and songs
black with mistakes.
They know what you mean.

You're not on drugs.
You're not singing to
get in their pants.
You see yourself dead.
You scream yourself hoarse.

Touch Control

He looked like M. Jagger
so I wanted his brief,
dead-eyed, crossing-the-
street-with-a-portable-
radio-tuned-to-rock life.
He knew what I wanted,
someone dazed who'd peel
for a fistful of dollars.
He leaned against a wall
in deepest Hollywood.
That meant yours, whoever.
I watched him awhile, liked
his body, how poorly he
moved, apparently stoned.
He'll die young, I said
to revv myself up, then
crossed Selma Avenue.
He saw me, glanced away,
said, "He's too young, just
passing through," but I stop
before him, ask if he's busy.
He gets the idea, says No.
Then we're heading to my car
and everyone knows I'm using.
He's a regular, gets winked
at, sways like a dream
of Jagger drunk, eyes cast
a few feet into the mystic
all the way to Bel Air
and I make him feel just
like heroin, head twisting
wildly and mind flipped
at my touch like an animal's,
like Led Zeppelin's pounding
before him onstage at the
Fabulous Forum—one of the
great things in his life.

No God
for Michael Silverblatt

Sometimes I go to the pornos,
look through films for a face
I remember from youth, grow
distracted, drive the street
till I find it drawn in shadow

over another, open my car door
and swipe love. My Mercedes
still smells empty seven years
later. The dust from a thousand
big hiking boots, tennies and

sandals blurs softly into the
fur at the foot of the seat
nearest my side, where guys have
enthroned themselves for long
drives, slouched in the vinyl,

having gazed inside from the
sidewalk, like into a wishing
well. I parted the traffic
tonight, prowled for a young
man who looked like a shadow,

saw this guy staring straight
through me, swaying downtown
in loose jeans, with something
vague on his mind. He'll go
with me, do what I do. Nothing

else interests him this side
of death. Like me he's just
moving farther away. I can give
him a ride there, because my
route takes me over his haunt

like a man who, so long ago,
gathered livestock lost in the
snow, ran out of gas and froze
going home. We touch in a black
car, on a back road, until numb.

The Tenderness of the Wolves

1. Private World

Boys learn to walk. Soon they're gripping each foot
fall. Days peak at dead ends, around dancing. They
try to yell until their buck teeth are flames, then
sip icy beers. In the same city a man schemes. He
has grown from a boy to a man, to tenth power. He
can see through small clothing or, if not view,
sense. He remembers scenes in gym classes long ago.
He hates himself for not wrestling then. There are
boys waiting at the usual place for a girl, for a
man without knowing it. Their heads are flipped
back in laughter. Even when they sleep or space-out
on drugs, rock music remains in their lives. A black
flag of it rules the unconscious. It draws their
ideas crudely around them. It is their power. They
are animals. The man remembers youth well. His
viewpoint so fierce and monochromatic, like music's,
that boys are drawn closer. They line the school
wall sewing joints with their spit, waiting for
godhead. They hear this man's rap and break rank,
stumble after. They'd crawl nude across fire, blind-
folded with ropes around their necks for a powerful
sensation. The man realizes and offers them cocaine
then women or violence, the heaven that they under-
stand. So they enter his version, through lungs
and big noses. Rooms spin and highs deepen. They
pass out together in chairs, across tables, joints
still in their kissers. Then the man walks among
them rubbing his eyes as if dreaming, for the world
appears like Guyana, but is heavenly warm.

2. Grip

While raping a boy
slide your hands
around his neck
closing your grip
until he is dead.

And that feeling
stays with you
forever, knowing
you used what he
had then undid it.

Now let the news-
papers take over
and show you
his past and its
promise, his power.

He increases in
value with death
until all young
girls clutch pens
rhyming tributes,

until women kneel
folding up hands,
until even the ones
who despised him
desire him, press

palms into crotches,
his damp open hands
holding onto the girls,
being held on the earth
in a powerful grip.

3. Darkens

He orbits a hobby horse laughing. His life catches the
over head light. He spins so fast the wind keeps him
clean. There is a kid who likes watching him. He is
the boyfriend of someone important. He would be missed
in a minute. There is a wife in his tarot cards. His
breakfast table is well over-stocked, the food bright
as headlights aimed up. Now his body fills out like
his father's. He towers over his schoolmates. They
meet him then ache through their bodies. They want to
be where love's leashed to the crossbars. They want
to see it transferred to friendship, to lust or a trophy.
There is a worn out boy mid-admirers. I am that man,
looking backwards. I can't explain my attraction.
Need love, love power, seek children. And one shines
from the pack, well lit by attention, well built by
his parents. I hire him to clean up my work room.
I slip a pill in his deep breathing mouth. I sculpt
a hug into raping. I completely unravel his talent.
I take a knife to its history of power. And then its
world enters the river's. He winning that cold blue
reward. His body softens there, darkens and scrawls.
First he's impeccable, tense, too ideal. Then he is
weeping, annoys me. Then limp, cool, unprevailable,
dull. Then sprawled saint-like on the floor, gazing
upward. I dump that in the river and he is gone.

4. An Aerial View

When God thinks, "Your turn,"
light soaks the grass in your pipe,
hat's pulled down over your head
and you groove into the ground.

And then He is confused:
"Did I make the right decision?
Was the child an appropriate scapegoat?
What did it do to deserve this?"

His anonymous, grey head
drops in puffy, shopworn hands:
the palms of a diletante
who does his work by suggestion.

He loves the glimmering earth.
He loves all that springs upon it.
He hates to slip one thing into darkness.
Thus, when He does, He is tortured.

He is bored, pissed, feeling strange,
His eyes hard to read clearly,
His hips dark with a longing;
a child dims where it's beaten.

He is amused and then guilty.
His lips are lava which has cooled,
His mind as wild as the tree tops,
as dope touched to match, breath.

5. Late Friends
for Robert Piest

They knew you were born to win the Olympics 'cos once,
crossing the quad at school, they saw a spotlight fall
out of the noon, traced its gaze to the gym, through a
skylight, where you practiced as gymnast. At first you
seemed heroic, but talking with you saw your limits: the
sports world, one primitive concept. You never gave War-
hol a chance. And with all your movement came muscle,
then to that the eyes of dark strangers. Once, after work,
someone tails you. You are raped, strangled and dropped
in the Des Plaines River. The man who does it feels
spiritual and light. Your friends are down wind at the
high school: doused faces, dim shouldered. Aliens where
jocks fire up taller and stronger each day. The girls
dream of you on the crossbars. They saw you naked;
they can see what he did to you. Guys will never touch
the Des Plaines again until you are pulled out, wrapped
in a black towel and the light goes on under the ripples
again. Then they'll water ski. First, friends heard
you had run away and pictured you well lit, neck deep
in blue ribbons. But then they found out how you slither,
a grey stretched out version of you mixed in with the
fishing. Now they doff their good sense in remembrance,
quit night jobs, drop classes. Grades spin in their
upper right hand corner like a slot machine's. It only
lets up when they talk with each other, your name on
their lips, in whispers. It's simple to turn those to
kisses. While you turn endlessly in water beneath the
world, your pals are behind, dating your girlfriends,
seduced by your buddies. They french and roll across the
things that you loved, like they're putting out fire.

2.

A Herd

1.

When a bell rang to signal their lunch was over, sixty or so of the high school's students strolled toward the gym and its locker rooms, boys into one, girls in the other. Four parallel rows of green lockers crowded with young men, shoulder to shoulder, yanking sweaters over their heads, popping shirts open and crushing them in small wads. These were tossed in dark cubbys and replaced on their bodies by grey teeshirts emblazoned with crude block letters: Smith, Wojnarowicz, Peters, etc. Then they slipped similar shorts up their legs and over jockstraps which had been snapped on the asses of friends, for kicks, before wearing.

With tennies and socks bunched under one arm, they rushed out to the basketball court, slipped them on there, stood in organized, memorized rows and swore at or punched one another. The coach jogged from his office, paused some distance away with his legs apart, hands on hips, bit a whistle tight in his teeth and toot! The boys stood straight and yelped their names in alphabetical order from front to back, twelfth to tenth grade, low to high pitch.

The coach clapped his hands as he rattled off "jumping jacks", "sit-ups", "leg-lifts", "push-ups" until the boys panted. Their chests stuck to their shirt fronts. Thin lines of sweat flared up in the cracks of fat asses. The whistle fired twice and they crowded onto the track for three laps, while the coach wrote in his book by each name, marking how far they'd run since the first whistle blew.

"Now," the coach said to his rabble, "there's baseball, football or tennis. I expect you to do something. Don't sit around." They divided into groups of two or three and streaked to their particulars.

Two of the scrawny ones squatted down by the gym with paperback books, their heads lowered. Three others joined them. Coach Wilson watched, swept the sweat from his face and wagged his new crewcut. "If they want D's they'll get them."

"I'd have them in for detention," his junior coach snarled. "Fucking twerps."

"Well, my own son is like them. I guess they just don't want to look incompetent. They'll regret it when they're my age and flabby. But for now, I figure, I'll let it go." He shrugged and walked toward a slew of boys tossing a football.

"Over here," he shouted, and one kid fired it to him. "Over

there, Jawinsky," he yelled and sent it back two feet in front of the diving boy. The other kids laughed at their friend's misfortune and the coach felt admired. "Okay," he said, "let's make something of this. I don't have to remind you." The boys picked teams then formed into shapes, lines. They crashed into each other for the bulk of the hour.

Five boys snuck to the empty coke stand near the bleachers, crouched down in its center and passed a fat joint around. The dark, cool realm of the stand had the privacy of afterschool hours. They could relax there and talk. Sometimes a kid would rush up, a.w.o.l. from some ballgame, to buy a few joints for his team. Only once or so in a year would a baseball drop in, hit by some slugger, and force them out of their foxhole.

When one of their members vanished from school, snagged by police, as one or two were every year, other students barely noticed. These boys were so vaguely impressed in the general view. They remained stoned, standing or rocking from heels to toes in front of various backdrops. Or they were statues, tilted back on school walls, whispering deals to the passers. They were less than students, more like fixtures off in the corners of eyes. It was so easy to miss them, wherever they were.

Jay Levin did most of the stand's heavy dealing. He had blond hair which spilled from a careless zig zag down head-center and fell in split ends which brushed off his shoulders when he walked around. His face was a nondescript, pimply white, ruled by blue bloodshot eyes. His smile starred a gold tooth where his parents couldn't afford perfect capping. He was known around school for his kindness. When poor kids approached him with pockets turned out, he would grin and tilt his head slightly. "It's good stuff," he'd say, more often than not, then slide a free baggie of pills from his wallet.

When Frank, the big dumb kid in Jay's gang, didn't show up at school for a week, most kids who noticed at all told the obvious jokes about where he'd passed out. But Jay and his friends plunked their bewildered expressions with hash pipes and tried to locate him. Banned from his afterschool life by his parents, they couldn't call up to ask how he was. All they could do was smoke and imagine. And after a month they agreed that he must have entered the army or something. He became sort of a legend to them.

But when Jay didn't show up at school for a while, his friends couldn't give up on him. He was their leader. They spread the word around campus. None of Jay's buyers had seen him. Now great crowds were alarmed. One industrious group of Jay's distant customers made up a flyer and stapled it to the phone poles at school. Two of Jay's more mystical contacts held a seance to find out if he was a ghost and could tell them. But the details were too complicated. They wound up just getting stoned and playing his favorite records. Even the coaches, most of whom bought the odd joint off of Jay, cared enough to phone the police and discovered they'd already searched themselves out.

2.

When a boy was undressing in his room, after a full day of school, his homework, a meal and a single smoked joint, he was relaxed. And if he was watched through a window, cut in three parts by the partly closed shades, by a viewer who had nothing gentle or worthy to do, it was very much like that boy was performing a striptease, although he paid no attention to what he was doing, and how, and in what order his clothes hit the carpet, or in what direction he faced. Everything was seen and judged from the window. It was as if when the boy turned away or walked for a moment behind his desk chair, obscuring his hips, it was done for a reason.

The man outside mulled an aesthetic to fit the occasion and fashioned rewards from these limits. He decided the one desk lamp was lighting as reasoned as Nestor Almendros'. The set of the bedroom indicated what was to follow. The bed was an obvious lead. The clothes in the closet were a bevy of levels to paw through and decipher for clues to this naked young fellow. And so on.

The man crouched in the dark, with leaves stuck to his clothes. There was no watch dog or it had been stilled in some fashion. It was too late at night for the mother to stroll out and garden, or for the father to hose down the driveway. Whatever brothers or sisters this boy may have had were tucked away and unconscious or bringing their tiny holes and penises to fruition in ways much too simple to worry about. This boy was old enough to know what lay in his body and how to make it his slave. He pulled off his teeshirt. He yanked down his slacks with his underpants in them like cream in cool coffee. Then he sat on the edge of the bed, used his hands to tow himself into its center. The boy touched his cock, got it hard. The man joined in for his part. He judged the slightest veer from tradition. When the boy twisted his head to the right, sucked the skin on his shoulder, the boy believed it belonged to a beautiful girl. The man saw what it was—a young man kissing his own skin—and every move or jerk after was richer.

If the boy was joined by a girl it was greater to kneel before them in the soft dirt outside. The girl could, via her range of expressions, tell the man what he should be feeling while watching the boy. The girl lay flat on her back or on her side. Her face was all pleasure. The boy hunched by her, head to head, head to crotch and finally rocking on her, letting a few lines of feeling seep past his tightly held jaw and fierce eyes. In this way, he was farther away from the man when he was with her. The man saw more of the body but less of the boy.

But if the boy was joined by a boy, the man had peered in a pond stocked with treasure. There was a second child, maybe as handsome or more than the first. And neither just lay there. Neither one showed enough pleasure for two, or just looked determined to turn his partner into a writhing mass of expression. The man imagined himself in both bodies, sharing the wealth. Or he could smash this window and join them, feel more than his share, have it all to himself. This was the best way to see the boy. This was the heaven that seemed to exist only at night through windows clouded with a man's breath. The man threw his head back and forgot the boy, came on himself. He needed only his hands.

The boy wiped himself off with a stiff towel which he tucked under the bed. The man let his cum lie, slipped it back in his pants. The boy touched the lamp and disappeared. The man had to duck down so his shadow, just scarcely there in the street light, wouldn't cross the boy's kingdom and frighten the king. He walked a long while, past the houses he'd looked at before, ones too dark to hold riches. They were darker yet now. At the end of a street lined with cars, his waited, one of hundreds. He drove across town. Nothing mattered to him now but sleep.

3.

The woods were dark and cool at all times. They invited people in at their edges. But miles and miles deeper they stretched and congealed. No one went there. Animals retraced their steps for this or that foggy belief. Little else knew or availed itself of that beauty. Someone would stagger in lost, starving or wounded, fall and die then disappear into animals' mouths. Then, one day much later, maybe men would hike in and carry away the white sketch left behind. They would speak angrily but nothing around them could understand. So they left things as they were.

If there was a God, He would have liked to lift the cities up in the air with a wave of huge hand and plunge them into the woods, leave them there a month then drop them back at their seasides and in their valleys. He liked the idea of that mixture and grew tired of both the cities' sharpness and the woods' sleep. Wake the woods up, calm the cities down. But He couldn't do this, for unknown reasons. He could only pour rain on the buildings, or snow when He was angry. And into the woods He pointed a hunter once in a while, to stick a sharp pin in its side.

He leaned way over and looked at the town where Bruce lived. A white car was taking uninteresting young men inside it, then driving them to a tract house which God had to mark with an X to remember. The man who drove the car was as happy as humans could be. Deep in the house, he turned boys over and over like things on a fire. And examined them. And opened them up. The man was learning real secrets and he was growing too powerful. God was jealous. Stripping a boy, killing him would not give God much pleasure. Humans were small. God would have to look through a spyglass until His arm ached.

God wanted to cover this city with ice but thought better of it. Slow down, He told Himself. God lifted the roof off the man's house while he was busy over his victim. There was the man rummaging through a drawer full of tiny sharp objects. God barely understood them. There was the boy covered with blood. There they were together making love. God lowered the roof in its niche. He leaned back until the house, then its city became a small dot on the earth. Less than a dot. The earth was a dot, the most interesting one of the planets. God was flying backward through space, arms and legs stretched out before him like streamers. He looked a little like Martin Balsam when he flailed the front stairs in *Psycho*. But God was laughing, not shrieking. And that was how he would stay.

4.

Ray Sexton stayed in bed all day, then into the evening. He handled a newspaper slowly, reading everything scary. Occasionally, he shoved his hand in a bag of Doritos and brought back a dull yellow flower of them for his mouth. Tiny burnt chips slipped in unnoticed. His nose squinched up at those handfuls, but he swallowed all down.

The bedroom's decor was phony plush, like the rest of the house, with an assortment of prints, knick-knacks and furniture which appeared less expensive than they really were. The dresser drawers, picture frames and tables were pieces of plumed, baroquely cut oak, branded a greenish grey color which made everything in his house appear to have a five o'clock shadow.

It was 10:00 and Ray hadn't eaten a full meal since lunch, so he walked to the kitchen. He picked the thick mud-like goop in a plastic jar from the freezer. He licked a chunk off the serving spoon, let it melt on his tongue, drift down his throat and off into blubber. He thought about boys, those he'd seen today thumbing beachward with tee-shirts torn off at their ribs, as was a popular fashion. Too bad they'd been ugly.

Available boys were the dregs. He had to look hard at them for a smart pair of eyes or a sexy mouth. He'd gaze through the acne like a peeping tom would through thick bushes. When he had his way, he imagined them as the kids in the teen magazines he picked up at the market. Those magazine's stars were Ray's angels, freed from the limits of I.Q.s and coordination, whose distant looks had a cloudy, quaalude effect. Teen stars' perfection haunted him and a vague resemblance to one or another could, more often than not, be gleaned from the face of a boy he had killed.

A boy chained up or tied down, in the midst of whatever torture, might turn his head sideways and an idol's look would appear in one feature or other. When Ray was lucky it showed across a whole face, as if by magic, as though pulled out of a hat. More often, he wouldn't see the resemblance until the boy died. Then, with the facial expressions dulled and in place, he would gradually find that the kid brought to mind some ripe child whose hit songs were stuck on the radio's dials, whose visage beamed down from most billboards. Then, what Ray had done took on meaning.

Ray scraped out the last of the ice cream, executed a perfect layup of the carton into the sink. "Like that last boy," he remembered, "so easy to bring down." He had grabbed a youth from behind, plunged a full hypodermic of sleep into his arm.

Down in the basement, the unconscious youth had been strapped hand and foot on a table. When the body was naked, he swept the long hair from its face and no perfect being emerged. Although Ray squinted and imagined hard, no angel would fit on the cheek bones or lounge in the eyes. So Ray brought out the full-headed mask, gathered the hair into a wad at the top of the head so the piece would fit snugly. He zipped it tight up the back. He unzipped the eye holes and liked the lids which he found there, thought what he recalled of their masters was pleasant. He unzipped the mouth hole. He thought the lips were kissable on their own.

The body was white and smooth. The mask, which came to a halt at the Adam's apple, was black and rough like the head of a boy who, sad as he'd ever grown, had stuck his head in a campfire and lived on hairless, earless, his features a hardened blur. Ray's hands worried over the body from shoulders to feet. The mask was a shadow which had been focused down on the trouble spot, as black as a spotlight was bright. He pressed and pulled the boy's flesh, massaged as though giving pleasure, although the youth's senses stayed seamless, the sprawl undisturbed, the cock soft. His mouth joined in and a real tenderness started to temper his actions. It rose out of nowhere. Ray loved being this close to a young body, smelling its haplessness and using it as a lover. Then, when he grew sick of this surface and needed to know how it curved so and what it could say, he'd want to destroy it and he would say loudly enough so that someone, if nearby, could hear, "No one else will have this pleasure."

Ray's breaths were quick, wordy. The boy's were spaced out and hollow. Ray had his arms underneath the body, embracing the boy, whispering throatfuls of praise. He crawled on top, spring his cock from its slacks and rubbed it along the flat belly. His tongue traced the shoulders' supports. He rested his cheek in a wet spot he'd made.

He lifted his head and looked in the eye holes, at the pink lids. He gazed at the mouth. It seemed as soft as the lips of one of his idols, and just the same shape. Ray lifted the head bundle up, lowered his own. He kissed, licked and shoved his tongue down inside for a while, then withdrew. All that motion had left the lips parted, teeth slightly ajar. And there, flawing the view, lodged inside, was a gold tooth. Ray remembered it now, like a fart when the boy had first spoken.

"Shit!" Ray whispered, and zipped the slot tight.

Now Ray stretched on the bed. A glance at the clock showed time had wandered past midnight. He felt calm, for once, and would slip into sleep. One hand lay on the pillow, squeezing it gently. He thought about the backs of boy's necks where the haircut stopped and a soft trace of it trailed just a bit down the skin. He'd place his hand there with fingers resting behind the ears, caressing there as a man does a dog, to relax it. A dog's mouth would drop open and tongue plop over its edge. A boy's lips would moisten, swing around as though guided by radar, leak their tongue and its peace.

5.

Jay Levin was asleep at 9 p.m., as though he'd been stumbling around in a drug cloud all day, trapped in the haze and, finding himself finally inside the shape of a home, was quickly soluble there, then inert.

Jay lay on his back. The lights were on in the room. It was 11:30 p.m. He was asleep again. He had woken up, seen as much as he wanted of real life, and dropped off. Now it was 2 a.m. and he was imbedded again, deeper than ever. The same man wandered the room all night, unnoticed by the young man, like the slightest breeze. Jay had sensed busy hands, the smear of a mouth, one short insistent cock.

Jay fell on his back. He raised his head and looked toward a noise. A man was divvying through a large wooden chest, seaching for something. The boy couldn't raise up further. Why? He lifted one limp arm toward the man. The man turned, plunged in a needle. The boy's hand dropped and he was asleep again.

The man sat on the basement stairs. A boy slept on a table across the room. The man was deciding what to do next. He had made so much love to the boy, in such depth and detail that the boy wished to die right now. No, the man wanted him to die. With a boy like this, asleep and all, it was too easy to read thoughts into his head.

The boy had been terrified once and screamed like a soldier with bayonet out, bound hand and foot, sure he could box from its grip. "When I break out of these," he'd glared at the man, "you'll be a dead man." But he couldn't undo them. Then he grew sad, and was just as beautiful numb. He slept. He kept jerking out of his sleep, feeling something too huge in his ass. He fought it a while, made it worse and conked out.

Ray knew this boy. "Under these circumstances," he'd tell a group of the kid's friends, "Jay would scream until he was ugly, and pass out." He'd say it with such conviction that the friends would just stare at their hands, scuff their shoes on the ground and agree. He'd face the girls who had slept with the boy, toss them a few easy questions like "What does he do when you blow him?" and "How much hair in his ass?" They'd pipe up the answers and think the man jealous. Then he'd narrow his eyes and ask, "When you hack off his balls with a knife, and slap his face to keep him aware, does he scream for God or his mother? Or can you, by that point, understand what he says, the way the drugs slur up his speech?"

Ray had blood on his hands, on his pants where he'd wiped them. What to do with the sleeping thing there on the table. It was well known. It had been translated into Ray's language. It kept hiding from him in its sleep. There, such handiwork, and no one to show it to. So Ray woke the once handsome protrusion at one end of the thing a last time, to make sure it was proud of its new look.

The man surveyed it. He felt like a chef on t.v. He folded his arms, stared to where cameras would aim and, further behind, toward an imagined crowd of old ladies, their faces as moved as withered ones get, taking notes, planning to clone his feast in their homes. He looked down on the earth. It was ravaged.

"It's time," he said, "to alter this."

The man dumped the last of a pitcher of ice water on the boy's face. It turned but didn't open. He slapped its sides. He leaned down and screamed in its ears. It twitched and rolled. He shook the curly pate, slapped it again. It opened. It had nothing to say. Ray lay the pitcher on one side under it, so it could look down its body, or give the illusion of doing so.

"Goodbye, child."

Ray frenched the mouth. He picked up an axe. He chopped what was beneath him until no owner could claim it. Then he sat down on the stairs. 3 a.m. No boy haunted him. Or could. There was a woe unlike any present on earth, Ray thought. He couldn't stop staring through everything. As if he were a god, or were blind. More blind than a god, though he saw what he'd done.

By the time the sun had risen this high, 5:51 a.m., it held the windows, baked the curtains and was, by the time it found Ray, light as the touch of a guard on one dozing. Ray was tired but he was looking through the wallet of someone who didn't exist. It was owned by a boy who'd stood with another in front of a drug store and smiled at the camera. Once he'd been thirteen years old and was hiking somewhere. Here was a shot of a girl. Its back was signed "love". She must have slept with him. Ray peered in her eyes. She looked angry. Here was the older boy Ray recognized, dressed in his teeshirt and jeans at some rock festival. Ray flipped it by, couldn't look at it. Too soon after. Here was a Mobil card. Thirty-three dollars. A dime for emergencies.

Ray picked up a pair of blue underwear. It had been worn by a boy until it resembled him. Ray would keep this, like a bouquet tossed by a bride, to wander deep in a drawer. It would show up on occasion and haunt him when he was looking for something essential. The jeans, jacket—car keys swiped out of its pocket—wallet, socks, shirt and adidas flopped into the fireplace and joined their owner in "nowhere".

Ray got in the boy's car and drove it for miles, parked it in an alley behind a clique of clothing stores still hours from fans. He fished a bus map out of his coat pocket. He looked in one direction and walked.

6.

Dead boys were floating up in the headlines, and now those were fading away under heels and in piles out of sight. Most were from Orville Wright High School, where Jay Levin had gone. Its students and teachers were dragging around with their eyes dimmed as artists' erasers. The Principal realized this had to stop. But, being an upper class teacher, all he could think of to combat death was mulling it through. So he had someone in his office mimeograph an announcement and deliver one to each home room. Teachers, scanning the pages just handed them, shrugged and turned to their classes.

"The Principal has declared that the final five minutes of first period today will be spent in a reflective silence, in memory of the deceased boys."

Students nodded or stared into space. When the clock touched 8:55 a.m., rows of shushed children pressed their heads down to a stack of their school books as though they'd been whispering something. They thought about records they owned, or beautiful friends. Or they conjured a shadowy herd of the victims. They closed their eyes and let themselves grow very somber, nearly asleep, until the bell rang, then scurried off to new classes.

Two coaches sat in an office, while the boys in second period gym dragged themselves out of their bright clothes, into their greys. One coach spoke to the other.

"Jim, where's that Durand boy you've been training? I haven't seen him around lately."

"He's missing."

"Are you afraid he might be in some trouble?"

"To be honest with you,"—Coach Wilson quit tying his shoe—"what with all these boys turning up dead, I'm very concerned."

"I don't blame you, but he's a big kid. He can defend himself."

"Probably so, but why hasn't he called? His parents say he just vanished. He hadn't been worried or angry. He was his usual self. He was here running the track, then he was seen at a gym down off Main Street. After that, nothing."

"I'm sure he's okay. Now let's get back to work."

"I'll be right there."

Coach Baxter jogged out. Coach Wilson laced his sneakers, picked up his clipboard and locked the door behind him. The other coach's boys were doing sit-ups. His stood around talking. Seeing their leader, they formed into lines, ready for a command. Thirty willing young faces.

"One of you turn into Robert Durand," he wanted to tell them. But he said, "Run in place," and they did.

7.

Jay hadn't shown in three days. His parents waited for two, then phoned his friends and police. Nothing. They went to visit the Pearsons, whose son had been missing a year, and whom the Levins had met through the drug busts their wild sons had shared. They got together most evenings, in a loose circle, arms all over each other. They whispered long repetitive prayers so full of Jay's and Frank's names that an English teacher would have grabbed her blue pencil and changed most to "him" and "that guy".

The last of Jay's gang met in the coke stand after sixth period on the fifth day. They moped in from the corners of school, threw their books hard against the wooden counters, squatted and looked imploringly from one to another. They weren't leaders. They weren't boys who could even deal with the haunt of one memorization for homework, much less a friend whose whereabouts couldn't be fathomed. Bruce knew a lot about movies. Maybe he could say something with meaning in it. Tim's carefulness had always impressed them. They might follow him deeper into themselves and survive. Miguel drove the gang everywhere that it fled or it flew. Maybe he should do something, swerve this crew back on the track.

They passed joint after joint. No one held up at a certain point so as to stay at least semi-alert and guide their ranks with a semblance of order. None of them knew how. Each hoped another would come up with powers no one had pegged him for. They smoked and stared. Then, when the dope was gone and the sun fell so low that the shadows they sat in chilled icy, they looked at each other bunching their knees to their chests with teeth chattering and, like even dumb animals would, stood up and left.

The boys and girls carrying bats and balls up the sidewalk, approaching the school's generous playground, saw the three boys who were having such trouble just crossing the field.

"Look at those guys," one girl sneered.

"Fucking losers," replied her best friend.

"Can you see them alive in ten years?"

"No way."

Now the two groups of kids crossed paths on the sidewalk. The gang's eyes had a cataract glaze and stared at unfixed points in the distance. The sporty kids glanced over their shoulders, saw nothing out there. They didn't know what these zombies were after, but it wasn't in sight.

"Those guys should just open their eyes," one girl later yelled at her steady boyfriend, from her position in left field to his at third base. "This isn't bad." She indicated the field, themselves, the stores around school. Then she punched her fist into her glove and bellowed to a boy at home plate, "Hit it out here, Jackson!" The kid at bat bowed, firmed his grip and struck out.

In the car, Miguel turned to his friends. "Where to?"

"Any ideas?" Bruce asked Tim.

"Not really. I guess we could go look for Jay, but I wouldn't know where."

"I'll put on some music," suggested Miguel. He pushed in a tape of The Who.

It was dialed loud. They could feel its bass line rumble their jaws. They slouched in corners of the car, rested their heads back and crooked their left arms up as if fingering frets on guitar necks. Their right hands held invisible picks between thumb and foregfinger, slashing the air just in front of their belts. If they weren't crazy, they were a band. If they were a band, they were one which lounged its career in rehearsal, down a long stretch of highway, on poorly lit stages, repeating the songs of the stars. But they grew content in that way and, after ten songs, when their hair matted in sweat and arms cramped, Miguel drove the sleepy bunch off. It didn't matter where. They just cruised for a while.

It was late night. One by one they were home. Each boy's parents heard him stagger in and glanced at the clock. 2 a.m. on a school night. Where had he been? But when they got up to ask, he'd just get sullen or violent. So, if they loved their son, which they probably did, they left him alone. Lying there, ears on his crashing around, they hoped that sleep, if anything left on the earth, might settle him down and rearrange this wild disarray, like some flowers, for them.

8.

At 2 a.m. the phone rang in the Levin's house. Mr. Levin lifted his head from the pillow. His wife slept soundly. He reached over her and snagged the phone on its third ring.

He tried to say, "Hello." It sounded more like a croak. He cleared his throat and said, "Yes?"

"Is this the Levin residence? Mr. Thomas Levin?"

"Right."

"I'm sorry to disturb you. This is Lt. Peterson of the West Los Angeles Police Department. We've found a body which matches the general description of your son. Could you possibly come down here this morning and check?"

Mr. Levin blinked at the clock. "Yes. I'll be there. You're on Federal, right?"

"Yes. Thank you, Mr. Levin. I'm very sorry to disturb you. Good night."

His wife had lifted her head up at one point but was sleeping again. "Jane?" He shook her shoulder. "Jane." She opened her eyes and he told her.

They crowded into the bathroom, applying cold water to shiny faces, bringing their haircuts to life in his comb and her brush. They were in their late forties but looked much older these days. Jay, their son, had been wasted the last several years, since he'd found drugs in eighth grade. His nature was still very sweet, but it was so ragged, a wilderness. The yard games which he and his father once couldn't stop playing were lost on him now. Long walks he'd shared with his mother were planted like interviews there in the house: "Where have you been?" "Around." "What are you thinking?" "Nothing." He'd gotten too stoned or whatever to answer.

Mr. Levin pulled on yesterday's suit. Mrs. Levin slipped on a loose dress. It wasn't until they were in the car that they felt what they had to.

"I just pray to God it's not Jay," she sighed, and folded her hands, pressed them against her chin.

He wanted to say that it wouldn't be, but it could be. No one knew yet. Not the police who stood over a body and bantered the Levins' good name. Not he, a man at the wheel, too tired to think about dying, or let it deter him. They drove in near silence the rest of the way. At stop lights he'd hold her hand and gaze at her. She would stare at his eyes. "I know," he'd say softly. But he didn't.

"The Levins?" A policeman walked up from behind. They'd paused at the main desk looking around for directions.

"Yes, sir," Mr. Levin replied.

"This way."

Mr. Levin had one arm around his wife's shoulders. Her arm surrounded his waist. Their limbs had moved there at some point on the drive. He noticed and turned to her. She glanced back. To him, she seemed so frightened. To her, he looked amazed. The policeman opened a door and followed them in.

"The Levins?" asked a man at a desk.

"Yes," they and the officer answered together.

"This way."

The four approached what was clearly a body, covered by a blue sheet in the room's center. Mr. Levin tightened his hold on his wife so as to protect her from it. He wondered what he felt. Nothing or numbness. The feeling was vague like the form they approached. The blue looked like water. Like a combination of cloth and water. Wet cloth. Now they stood above it. Blue cloth and the soft curves of a body.

"The tooth that's supposed to be gold is missing. Other than that it matches the description we have." The fourth man was speaking. Who was he? He lifted the sheet up at one end, then back, not without a feel for dramatics.

"No," Mr. Levin said. It was a boy with long hair like Jay's, a big nose like Jay's, maybe Jay's chin. But it was not Jay. "No, it's not him."

"Okay," the man said. He looked weary. This would mean more work for him. The boy was covered again. "He must be a runaway, then. I'm sorry to have brought you here. Good night." He pushed the body and table away, toward a dark part of the room.

"I'll lead you back," the policeman offered.

Mr. Levin asked questions as they went. It relaxed them all a little. ". . . and we'll call you when we find anything further." Mr. Levin liked the officer or, rather, how steady he was, speaking the lines with a firmness which he could admire even now.

In the car, Mr. Levin exhaled loudly, in relief. "Well, it wasn't Jay," he stated, just to say something.

"But the boy it was, the poor empty thing. . .so silent. . .more like a ghost than a young man, really. If it had been Jay in that condition this would have been hell."

"The officer said that the boy overdosed on too many drugs. They found him in an abandoned house. . . "

". . .like a ghost. . . "

". . .naked like that. They couldn't find clothes anywhere. But there were no signs of molestation." He paused. "He looked somewhat like Jay."

"But skinnier and his face looked crazy, not like Jay's at all."

He fit one arm around her. "Jane, it wasn't Jay. We should feel good about that." He believed she was acting indulgent and worried she'd reach for a drink when they arrived home. She'd wind up crying. "Let's go right to sleep when we get there. Sleep will wipe this away."

"I hope you're right."

He squeezed her then brought both hands back to the wheel. In the silence that followed they thought about Jay. Mr. Levin pictured a boy around twelve years of age, ten feet away, with his hands out waiting for his father to throw a ball. He threw it. Jay caught it and grinned. They didn't have to say they loved one another. The game had implied it. That ball flew back and forth as if tied with a note. It read "I love you", meant freshly each toss.

Now Mr. Levin saw Jay in his bedroom—the Jay who had disappeared. The boy looked tired. That genuine smile was still there but it grew too easily, stayed too long. He had told his son to turn in, that it was late, Jay had looked back intensely, as if at a text. An ashtray of stubbed joints between the boy's knees explained why.

"Jay," he'd said, "turn in." And, getting no response, he'd said it again, almost inaudibly and very tenderly, feeling so strange in the hold of that gaze.

"Turn in."

Jay reached out and pulled the chain on the light.

Mrs. Levin pictured Jay dead on a table, covered by a sheet in a city far away. People like she and Mr. Levin looked at his face, said, "No," and drove home. He'd look so light he could be blown on the floor with a sigh. He'd look so cold she would cover him with a blanket, then her coat. She'd wrap her arms around her shivering self and pore over him. His face was going to turn brown and flake from its bones like a sunburn, somewhere in the future when she had forgotten it. Now she saw the young stranger she'd glimpsed on the table. He existed to scare her. She screamed very sharply and started to cry.

"Jay!" She yelled for her son.

Mr. Levin pulled the car to the curb and reached for her.

9.

The theater lights were so dimmed that Bruce had to linger by one of its doors for several minutes until a sunnier outdoor image onscreen focused rows of seats from the darkness. He slid into one near the back and hung his legs over the chair in front of him.

Up there, a chauffeur was driving a fairly attractive brunette down a highway. She looked worried.

"Jeeves?" She leaned forward, close to his ear. "I said I wanted to go to my friend's house. This isn't the way."

"Relax," he growled, swiveling his head.

As usual, at least in the porno Bruce had seen, the man wasn't nearly as cute as the woman. Now he parked the car and turned to her.

"You and I can have more fun than you and your girlfriend."

"Ooh," she purred, "I'd been hoping you'd ask."

What unbelievable and sexist shit, Bruce thought.

The man helped himself into the back seat, undressed her and himself. They had sex in the usual ways, with the typical breathy rewards. Bruce was bored but he had an erection and waited for it to relax, so he could go home.

Lying in bed late that night, his tired eyes on a newscast, he remembered the sex he'd seen. Finally, when he was exhausted and off in his sheets, he could think of it as the powerful gesture it was. He thought of the actress, and of the actor made plain so that men in the dark could project themselves over him, like holograms onto an animatron. Then Bruce was masturbating. The naked girl was a springboard. He imagined kissing Jay. Here, where Jay could have no idea what Bruce needed, he brought his friend's body beside him. He plugged his cock in Jay's smile, then ass. A smooth palm played their parts.

Bruce came. When he opened his eyes, he was alone. Jay had swung down like a pendulum out of the indistinct ceiling, then flew out of sight as soon as Bruce wanted.

Ray Sexton saw what he could through a window. He knelt on damp, saucy ground, among cold ferns and drainage pipes. A slit in the curtain framed the room's light and Bruce's role in it. Ray stayed in his spot until the scene was switched off.

In the dark, Bruce pulled his pillow close to his chest, as though it were Jay. They rocked. His instincts told him to go find his friend wherever he was. But Bruce was afraid that by morning he'd feel as strong as he did before lust had invaded. He knew that the language of lovers was simple, like that of the primates. All words pointed in and meant joining in one sense or other. That wasn't for him.

He unwrapped himself from the pillow, fit it under his head. It would be nice, he admitted, if this were Jay's stomach or thigh and the black blur the world became this late at night could, like a white wall, be projected with elsewhere when he grew too bored. Then he turned his back on the room.

Walking gradually down the sidewalk to his car, when the chum of his hard-on had fled and he was alone, Ray would think of himself as a scared man, as what he was. Watching the boy just now, he hadn't wanted to lie beside him and stutter how much he admired youthful bodies, though that's how he felt. Instead, he wanted to screw the boy's ass with whatever he could keep hold of, until that body's one rest stop matched its frantic compadre, the face.

On nights like this, when he wished a boy into his grave but that boy still breathed and the dream-corpse popped like a bubble, Ray felt deeply apart and away. He'd cum, but wished he could draw it back into his body, go kill a boy and let it loose there. Things didn't feel sexy and when Ray wasn't horny or couldn't be, he was worthless. He thought about suicide. He was afraid there was another lifetime just after this one, where boys he'd killed had ganged up. They lingered for him in the darkest mood between the decision to live or to die. He wasn't sure what they could do to him once he was dead, but it would be monstrous.

Where was Ray's car? He'd walked blocks past it and turned with a shrug, headed back. "I'll live," he knew, with the same shrug.

It was a warm night. Bruce sweated in his sleep, even with the windows open a bit and a lone sheet crumpled down at his knees. He lay on his stomach, one leg crooked to the right, his ass open a crack, its odor overcast there like the least of bad breaths, someone's last.

In a different world Jay would lean down, holding his tongue until Bruce's essence was his to store and recall. Bruce would sleep through this or he would pretend and wish love were this way, implied by such sweetness of thought, more like a wisp of religion one stole from another's facade without breathing a word.

The man in the porn film would twist one soft edge of his mustache, leer at the infrared camera and silently smack his lips at such buttocks. He would reach down, slip one hand under each hip and lift Bruce's ass like the lid off of something, sniff to make sure it was clean then worm his tongue in.

Ray would cover his face with a rag full of chemical, send the boy deeper than ever. He might treat this ass gently at first, so that he'd like it and so that he'd know what he ruled. Then he'd try to tear it in half like a phone book, or center it in the sight of a shotgun. Awash in Ray's slopping of kerosene, Bruce would chill, start to wake up. Ray would step back. A lit match would Tinkerbelle down.

10.

Jay Levin dashed from the coke stand to locker room later than even his lazy friends had. By the time he'd snuck to his slot in the green metal rows, only a few of the stragglers lingered behind, tying the last of their shoes on. He'd be late for his next class, no matter how quickly he changed, so he simply relaxed, let it go.

He peeled off his stinking grey teeshirt, kicked his adidas and a tangle of jockstrap toward his compartment. The shower room was a white tiled chapel running along the right side of the lockers. Ten or so nozzles aimed down from each of five sparkling columns. He'd never done more than peer into that realm with amazement before, at the white bodies and steam which enhanced them. Now he stepped to a nozzle, grabbed its handles, twisted them and let out a yelp as the water nearly inhaled him, backside first. The rush slugged him between his pale shoulders. He sunk against the column and let the shower have him more fully, embrace and congratulate him.

"Fuck everything," he sighed aloud, as his long blond hair darkened and snaked down into his eyes.

Outside, it had started to rain. Jay stood in the entrance a while, hoping it would ease up. A jock in a teeshirt and shorts strolled up the walkway, not even trying to cover his head. Looking at him, Jay felt cold. And the jock, seeing the boy was unfriendly, wandered by mumbling incomprehensible threats. Finally, Jay ran up the direction the jock had come, into the parking lot. It had grown too late to go to his class, so he decided he'd drive into Hollywood, try to unload a few wads of his just-purchased kilo and just forget the whole rest of the day.

A load of boys were standing around on the sidewalks over a several mile stretch of Hollywood's dumpiest boulevard, in front of its bars and taco stands, selling the bulge in their pockets. Some had their thumbs half-heartedly out, so police couldn't snag them for loitering. Some just stood on the corners and scanned through slow moving cars. If young guys were driving, the scan was a leer. If an officer, or an old person, or family, the scan was indifferent. Those cars weren't going where boys were. Customers wandered the sidewalks, and dealers hissed out the luscious words "grass" or "hashish" to each passer. Some kids would stop, exchange greens, then follow the sellers to nearby parked cars.

Ray had searched everywhere for a victim that evening—chic Westwood, outside nightclubs, in pinball parlors. It was well after midnight. All respectable children were off in their beds. He'd have to wipe a kid off the boulevard. Boys there were easy. Because they were druggies, the worst was expected, so when cops found them dead they just heaved them straight in the ground. Ray had picked his earliest victims from its ranks, before he'd tested the high school's.

He was cruising it now. In the low light of street lamps and neon bar logos, the long haired boys glowed at first glance, like the young courtiers in Renaissance paintings which Ray had kissed as a child. By the third or fourth go-round, bright doorways and closer checks revealed age marks, scars and flaws in conception. A shimmering reef of red hair covered the mug of a pirate. What seemed a doll's face was hit by a headlight and looked like the man in the moon's. It was more than an hour before he saw one that he could imagine was decent. Even so, this face would gradually end up in the mask.

Ray's car, which had been rubbing the curb where Jay stood, came to a stop. He climbed out and approached, made an offer then followed the boy to a car parked on a side street, between two lamp posts, under a tree which would keep their transaction a secret. It made Ray's hypodermic seem like a magician's or doctor's swept out of his pocket and plunged in Jay's arm with an unnoticed flourish.

Hours later, at 4 a.m., when it had been dark long enough to bore nearly everyone on the earth into sleep, Ray carried a heavy, dusty bundle over his shoulder out of the basement up to the garage. He tossed it on the back seat of an auto. It was a carpet rolled around something. A boy's shaved head was just in one end like the fruit of a chapstick.

He drove the San Diego Freeway beyond the Sepulveda Pass into the suburbs. The offramp at Ventura Blvd. was empty and, on its left side, bracing the hill back up to the freeway, thick trees suggested a wilderness. But the illusion halted abruptly behind them, at a rocky grey slope. When Ray parked the car, clawed through the foliage and found a spot for his refuse, he was surprised to learn that the earth still felt warm. Like skin, he realized, just after death when there was no hint of the sentence passed over it.

Ray sprawled out in the mixture of moonlight—far left—and the sun—far right—catching his breath at one end of the carpet. The boy perched on the other, as cold as a sculpture which Ray had stolen from some art museum and broken. It was worthless to him and to them. All he could do was to dump it somewhere. With a kick of his shoe it slid down the dirt and lodged in the fleece of damp grass below.

When Ray had wallowed back through the bushes, he looked behind him and saw how secret this place seemed. He thought how the corpse might stay hidden, a distant white blur to the hurrying drivers, like their expressions in choppy pond water. It was a sight which would smear in the mind, be erased by the long straight freeway, grow vague as the date, as the night would become, then the month and everything not photographed in it.

11.

"Dear Mother,

I'm dead. That was me in the abandoned house. I fooled them. You can sleep now. I don't think I miss you, but I thank you for all that you've..."

The paper flew out of her hands. It twisted and skidded across an empty parking lot. She couldn't chase it fast enough. When she tripped and fell she found Jay prone beneath her. He looked like the boy she'd seen on the table.

"He's still alive," she realized, and got to her feet. She ran toward a warehouse. Its door was open and Tom was inside. She looked back over her shoulder. Jay had stood up. She turned and ran at him. Halfway there, she woke up.

It was morning. Mr. Levin was showering. She was covered with sweat.

"Jay's alive," she whispered. Then she felt crazed for believing her dream. "God help me," she sighed. And He did.

A car had broken down on a freeway. Its driver and passenger stood around, waiting for someone to help them. The sun made everything sparkle. In its midst, the taller one narrowed his eyes. He was looking over the edge, toward an offramp. There was something down in the bushes. They agreed, then skidded down on their shoes and their hands.

It was Jay.

Bruce sat behind Tim; Miguel steered. They kept their sights over the five cars ahead of them, on the black one. Jay was inside it. They'd blathered about his death at school. Sadness had passed mouth to mouth, like mono. It showed in their car, which was usually swerving but now nearly towed.

The Levins followed the hearse. This time the body they'd checked on was theirs, and it hadn't been cool and collected like that other boy's. Murder had changed it. They had to gawk at their son just to see him. First he'd been molested. Then he'd been chopped up and dropped by a freeway. That's all they knew or wanted to know.

Mr. Levin was angry, strangling the wheel. Mrs. Levin was calmer. She just wished they were burying her dumb, white boy and not that creature who once had been Jay. What situated itself in that black car scared her. When she imagined, as she did, the lid of the coffin raising up, something crawled out and attacked her. If that ruined Jay was to rise from its box and try to get home she would ask her husband to pull his gun from the bedside table and shoot it.

"Into the ground, that's where a coffin fits. It doesn't belong out here. The earth's sharks," thought Bruce, surveying the graveyard, each flat white stone like a buoy warning of who was below. He scanned the hundreds of students in a dense ring around Jay and his parents. Bruce had passed most of them in the hallways at school. But in these black suits, with their loud mouths shut down and eyes lowered, they seemed to be actors who'd played those wilder roles.

The priest stopped intoning and waved his hand at Jay's father. Miguel squinted to look at the man. He looked a lot like Jay would have if he'd made it into his forties.

Mr. Levin unfolded a sheet of paper from his suit coat pocket. "I want to read something," he said, "which is the lyric to a song Jay and I used to listen to when he was a boy. It was a favorite song of mine. I didn't think he understood what it meant, but not long ago he heard me playing it and told me he'd known that it said a lot about my feelings for him and, indirectly, his for me."

He looked at the young mourning faces. For a moment he thought he might have made a mistake. This was an old song. Maybe these youngsters would laugh at it. But their faces looked up at his, he decided, with curiosity and respect.

"When I was seventeen, it was a very good year. It was a very good year for. . ."

"Oh God," Tim thought, hearing the words his own father sung along with when they crossed the radio. It was the song of an old man and not of a boy. Tim pursed his lips. How selfish of this man to pick a lyric which Jay didn't care about. When someone's a child, he listens to what his god plays. So it was conceivable that Jay recognized this song and, out of the kindness he had been known for, shared his dad's mood. But Mr. Levin should have remembered how young his son was and been more alert. Tim didn't expect him to read words by Jimi Hendrix, but these were so far from Jay. Jay would never be old enough to express them.

"When I was twenty-one, it was a very good year. It was a very good year for small town girls who lived up the stairs, with perfumed hair which came undone, when I was twenty-one."

Bruce stood beside Tim. The fact of the song's inappropriateness hadn't occurred to him. He thought of how powerful the lyric was, in its archaic way. Jay's father was reading in the exact tempo of the Sinatra version. Bruce could imagine an orchestra swelled up behind. He pictured Jay's face, exhaling these lyrics with dope smoke. Then he tried to remember the shape of Jay's body, in gym, at the moment his hero had stood between grey shorts and jeans. He knew what he'd felt for it. Love, he'd decided, though he was too loaded to say now for sure.

Mr. Levin stopped reading and took one step back, instinctively, as he had in the army, to show he was finished. The priest unfolded his hands and began to speak about what Jay had meant. His voice was a rosy old drone which sent each mourner off into his or her daydreams until the sermon was less than a negligible backbeat herding them on. He lowered his voice for the final few words and the funeral ended.

The friends of Jay's which the Levins approved of, came up to them to join hands. People embraced one another. Death was vague, like the idea of God, but it somehow informed that to hug a good friend, thereby turning one's back on its captive, was the only way out.

Bruce took Tim and Miguel in his arms. They looked so loaded to him. Once, when he'd been on mescaline, Bruce had decided that if he drank orange juice each morning he'd never feel lonely again. Now he gazed in Tim's bloodshot eyes, then Miguel's, and thought that if he looked in them every day he'd stay happy.

The Levins shook every hand which was open, then walked to their car, his arm around her, her weight on him. Jay's friends fanned into the evening. Bruce, Tim and Miguel drove to the coke stand and plowed themselves under the dope and the darkness.

When the crowd had all gone, some workmen with shovels strolled up the graveyard's green hill, slightly drunken, like dreams might approach sleeping heads. The coffin was waiting, its smooth brown surface as neat as a bedspread and nicer than what was inside. These men didn't know what and nor did they care. They said a few words to each other and dug their tools in the dirt.

12.

Ray Sexton lay in his bed. He'd been napping most of the day. To his right was the day's latest headline. Police had found another one of his victims. There was a photograph on the front page. "He didn't look like this," Ray said to himself. This one had his hair combed, was wearing a tux and was spruced-up for what Ray guessed was a prom. The boy Ray had fucked with was less of a "yes man" and dirtier, drowsier. Poring over the photo, Ray felt like a parent who'd made the mistake of gazing into a coffin, at the corpse of his son. This photo refocused Ray's vague idea of his victim. This was not what he'd killed.

There was a tenderness in the body, like there was the corpse of a beautiful boy in the ground. It lay that cold and far away, seen only by the hungriest eyes, the weepiest blue. When Ray thought of someone he needed, he felt empty. When he knew he'd get what he wanted he felt empty. In every cool body something could warm without reason. His hands would veer from his work and anchor him at the flesh. But when it grew cold he felt nothing. Before, he wanted it. Now it felt cold and empty.

Ray looked at the face of a boy in the newspaper. The young man had put his lips close to a camera, pouted. The camera had focused, flashed. The face had slid through a hole in its side, unfogging slowly. The face was reduced, on a page full of landscapes, all their homes burning and customers charred. There was the boy like a hostage among them. Ray wished he could hand this boy his photo to autograph. The boy would write "loved you, kissed me, I'm yours in your place, let's fade away" then his first name. It was printed below. Jay. It rose from death like a single bone from a tar pit.

Once that bone was a boy. It moved about freely amid some hysterical pinball machines, in cars sliced out of *Star Wars*. Pimples roamed his faces. He hugged girls closer than Ray could imagine. Arrogant scowls arched his eyebrows. He'd argue with girlfriends, get mad and walk home. Ray tore the picture out of the paper. He tacked it to a bulletin board, by the others. Five cute boys whom he'd known. A row of cute tilted heads that wished black and white photos were manholes which they could crawl out of. Five heads hung high by a hunter.

Where Ray stood, there was a smell which he'd sweetened with lysol and blown around the room with a portable fan. It had stayed, as if a ghost, as though it were lazy. Ray had noticed it two weeks ago in a spot in the hall and one by the sofa. He'd searched their shadows and just come up dusty. Then it had covered the house. He'd put bodies down in the crawl space, like beasts into a cage. Now they reached up and swiped at him through the floor boards.

For days, this odor had quashed his plans. The ideal had grown sour and he was left holding the bag and looking around for something to fill it. There had been nothing. Then, gradually, the longing came back. This new wrinkle and stink added force to it. It made boys seem even more delicate, midway between childhood and...—Ray swept his hand through the sickly air—...and this grotesquerie. He'd told the most recent boy to breathe deeply. "Know what that is?" he'd mused. That's where you're going." The boy had looked bewildered. It was a concept almost as vague as a heaven but, unlike God's campground, a boy could sniff this one and know it was real.

Ray flipped on the t.v. and stationed himself on the end of his bed. It was a console model, which Ray had acquired, as he had his whole house, with the money left him by his parents. They'd died when he was twenty, in the crash of a light plane. And now on the t.v. news a reporter was saying a plane had gone down just that morning. It seemed like one fell every day. Ray's loss was one of the millions.

The dead boy's face came on the screen. It stared several seconds, followed by a crude sketch of another found just a few days before, unidentified still. It didn't do the kid justice. Ray hadn't used the mask over him. The face was ground in his mind like a boot heel. The newscaster was saying police had linked up the murders. This was old news. They were looking around for the creature who'd done it.

"Good luck!" Ray exploded in laughter.

If there was a God, He watched this and wallowed. Not that He didn't have head colds to decongest elsewhere and better monsters on earth and in space, but he'd grown obsessed, for imperious reasons. The greed and resentment still perked in His eyes but His alternate choices were snuffing this interesting scene, which would be fruitless, or slipping some clue to police, and that would be meddling. Better, He knew, to let it go on as it had: incomprehensible, beautiful. God leaned down closer. There was the man in his window, acting just crazy. There were the lonely friends kneeling at edges of bedtimes, with prayers floating up and their faces cast down. What kind of logic was that, He wondered. "Let them be nothing." He watched a while longer, but prayers were the dull part and death the most boring of all. Enough for today. He let Himself drift slowly away like a freighter unloaded of all its cargo, with only His eyes on the man where he'd stopped for one final idea before dreaming.

Ray stood at the bedroom window, dead tired. With the darkness outside and the light on inside, it was a mirror. He'd remembered something deep in his past, a trick with the glass which his mother had taught him when he was much younger.

She'd positioned him so, turned the lights in the house off except for a candle she held a few inches under his chin. When he'd stared at his face a long time, not blinking, his features had softened and changed, grown scars, other hair, different noses and eyes. She'd said these were the faces he'd had in previous lives.

Either she'd been crazy or that candle special because there was nothing here now but exhaustion, as casually his as the sight of an ass in its dull slipshod jeans. Daylight would show up and scrub it away on red knees. Ray would see outside again, master boys, make them nothing. But first everything had to grow darker, be covered completely, make him shiver as he shivered now when he turned out the lamp's light and slept.

Biography

Dennis Cooper was born 1/10/53 in Pasadena, California, and grew up in nearby Covina, then Arcadia. He currently lives in West Los Angeles. He has one previous book of poems to his credit, *Idols* (The Sea Horse Press, 1979), and three chapbooks: *Tiger Beat* (Little Caesar Press, 1978), *Antoine Monnier* (Anon Press, 1978) and *The Terror of Earrings* (The Kinks Press, 1973). He is the editor and publisher of Little Caesar Magazine and Press; he put together the poetry anthology *Coming Attractions: American Poets in Their Twenties*, and coordinates the reading series at The Beyond Baroque Poetry Center in Venice, California.